CONNOR

BEDARD

HOCKEY SUPERSTAR

BY TODD KORTEMEIER

Book design by Jake Nordby
Cover design by Jake Nordby

Photographs ©: Charles Rex Arbogast/AP Images, cover, 1; Minas Panagiotakis/Getty Images Sport/Getty Images, 4, 7; Darren Calabrese/The Canadian Press/AP Images, 8–9, 21; Tom Pennington/Getty Images Sport/Getty Images, 10; Lawrence Scott/Getty Images Sport/Getty Images, 12, 16; Jonathan Kozub/Getty Images Sport/Getty Images, 14–15; Andy Devlin/Getty Images Sport/Getty Images, 18–19; Bruce Bennett/Getty Images Sport/Getty Images, 22; Justin Berl/Getty Images Sport/Getty Images, 25; George Walker IV/AP Images, 26, 30; Red Line Editorial, 29

Press Box Books, an imprint of Press Room Editions, Inc.

ISBN
978-1-63494-870-8 (library bound)
978-1-63494-888-3 (paperback)
978-1-63494-922-4 (epub)
978-1-63494-906-4 (hosted ebook)

Library of Congress Control Number: 2023922011

Distributed by North Star Editions, Inc.
2297 Waters Drive
Mendota Heights, MN 55120
www.northstareditions.com

Printed in the United States of America
042025

About the Author

Todd Kortemeier is a sportswriter and editor who has covered hockey for USAHockey.com and TeamUSA.org, including at the 2022 Winter Olympics in Beijing, China. A lifelong Chicago Blackhawks fan, he enjoys cheering the team on with his wife and daughter from his home in Minnesota.

TABLE OF CONTENTS

bauer
CANADA
16

1 MAKING HISTORY

Connor Bedard fired a shot, but Slovakia's goalie blocked it. The young center quickly got the puck back and went to work. First, he skated to the middle of the ice. Then he cut to his right, leaving a defender in the dust. Connor moved back to his left. Then an opportunity presented itself.

At just 17 years old, Connor was the youngest player on the ice at the 2023 World Junior Championship. He had already set records in the tournament.

Connor Bedard scored nine goals in seven games during the 2023 World Junior Championship.

But what he wanted most was to help Canada win gold. Now, in overtime of the quarterfinals, he had a chance to move his team one step closer to that goal.

Another Slovakia defender lowered his stick to the ice to block Connor's shot. But Connor used his quick hands to avoid the defender. Now he had only the goalie to beat.

Earlier in the game, Connor had scored a goal and assisted on another. Throughout the tournament, Connor had carried the hopes of his country on his back. But if Canada couldn't score the next goal, its tournament would be over.

MR. CLUTCH

Connor Bedard had developed a reputation for scoring game-winning goals. In his junior career with the Regina Pats, he scored five overtime game-winners. When he was 10, Connor scored a game-winner for his youth team in double overtime.

Connor Bedard celebrates his game-winning goal against Slovakia.

Slovakia's goalie dropped to his knees. However, the puck was still on Connor's stick. Connor pulled the puck back. Then he darted to his left and saw a wide-open goal. Using his backhand, he glided the puck into the net. The home crowd roared. Canada's next hockey superstar had lifted his team to the semifinals. And his record-breaking run was far from over.

GAME-WINNER

Overtime at World Juniors featured just three skaters on each team. That meant Connor beat almost the entire defense by himself to score the game-winner against Slovakia.

TELUS
BAUER
IIHF

2 THE FUTURE OF HOCKEY

Connor Bedard was born on July 17, 2005, in North Vancouver, British Columbia. The Bedard house changed once Connor started playing hockey. Connor had a stick in his hand by the age of three. He'd take his stick and a ball wherever he went around the house. The kitchen floor soon showed the scars of many stickhandling drills.

Soon after, Connor got on skates for the first time. Skating wasn't his favorite. But once he added a stick and a puck, he

Connor Bedard first played for the Canadian junior national team in 2021.

Connor Bedard showed exceptional skating skills from a young age.

became hooked. Soon he started imagining himself scoring goals to win the Stanley Cup.

Connor was also a talented soccer player. But by the age of 12, he mainly focused on hockey. The better he got, the more he had to practice and travel for the sport. Connor's father, Tom, worked as a logger. Tom traveled hours away from where the Bedards lived to get to his job. After a long day in the forest, Tom drove Connor to hockey practice. And on weekends, there was usually a tournament to go to.

Connor was often the star of those tournaments. His ability to handle the puck dazzled fans. No matter the defense, he seemed to cut right through and emerge with a chance to score. Canadian magazine *The Hockey News* called Connor the "Future of Hockey" when he was 13.

Connor dominated at each level of youth hockey.

ALWAYS THINKING HOCKEY

Once Connor decided to focus on hockey, the game took over his life. One time his family took a vacation to Hawaii. But Connor wasn't sure if he wanted to go. A week without hockey would be torture for him. As a compromise, Connor brought a stick and inline skates on the trip.

He often had to play against older, tougher competition. But it didn't matter. By the age of 14, he was ready for junior hockey.

Junior hockey leagues are usually filled with players in their upper teens. Some of them are college age. Fifteen-year-olds are allowed, but they're usually limited to just five games. Connor was different. He received special permission to play a full season in the Western Hockey League (WHL). He was only the seventh player in history to earn that honor.

The Regina Pats chose Connor with the first pick of the 2020 WHL draft. He wasn't even 15 yet. But Canadian hockey fans couldn't wait to see one of the country's most promising young talents.

Connor Bedard played three seasons with the Regina Pats.

98
CCM
P.P.C.L.I.
C
WHL
Pats
BAUER

16
BAUER

3 GOING GLOBAL

The 2020–21 WHL season lasted 24 games. Connor Bedard played in only 15 of them. During that time, he recorded 28 points. Connor could have played in more games. But instead, he joined the Canadian national team for the 2021 Under-18 World Championship.

Connor was the youngest player in the tournament. By this point, playing against older players didn't faze him. Connor scored two goals in the quarterfinals. Then in the semifinals, he netted a hat

Connor Bedard averaged more than a point per game in every junior tournament he played in.

trick. In the gold-medal game, he scored a goal and helped Canada win. Connor's 14 total points tied for the second-most in the tournament.

A few months later, Connor took part in the World Junior Championship. He became just the seventh 16-year-old in history to play for Canada. And it didn't take long for Connor to become the best scorer of those seven. In his first game of the tournament, Connor tallied four goals. Nobody, not even the legendary Wayne Gretzky, had scored that many as a 16-year-old.

Connor rejoined Regina during the 2021–22 season. With a year of experience, he scored often during his second season. He became

Connor Bedard helped lead Canada to the gold medal in the 2022 World Junior Championship.

the youngest player in WHL history to net 50 or more goals in a season.

In 2023, Canada called Connor again to play for the national team at the World Junior Championship. This time, he put together a record-setting performance. The highlight was his overtime winner against Slovakia. Two games later, Canada secured the gold medal in front of a thrilled home crowd. Connor was named the Most Valuable Player (MVP) of the tournament.

GIVING BLOOD, GIVING BACK

While with the Pats, Connor volunteered to help promote the Hockey Gives Blood program across Canada. The program encourages people to donate blood and stem cells to people in need. Connor met with patients battling serious illnesses.

The buzz about Connor had spread far and wide. He and the Pats played in front of sellout crowds wherever

Canada fans celebrate with Connor Bedard after the gold-medal game of the 2023 World Junior Championship.

they went. Almost every night, fans got to see Connor make an amazing play. In 57 games, Connor scored 71 goals and tallied 72 assists. No player had scored that many points in the WHL since 1996. It became clear that Connor needed to play against better competition. He was ready to face off against the best players in the world.

98

4 THE NEXT LEVEL

While Connor Bedard was lighting up the WHL, National Hockey League (NHL) teams were doing what they could to draft him in 2023. The more a team lost, the better chance it had to get the first overall draft pick. The Chicago Blackhawks ended up being that lucky team.

Before the draft even took place, fans in Chicago were thrilled to have the top pick. The Blackhawks made it official that June when they drafted Bedard. They

Bedard puts on a Blackhawks jersey after being drafted by Chicago.

saw a complete player. He was a great skater and had an elite shot. The Blackhawks planned to build their roster around Bedard for years to come.

Bedard didn't turn 18 until after the draft. It's rare for a player to be ready for the NHL at that age. But scouts considered him a once-in-a-generation talent. Many fans compared Bedard to Connor McDavid. Like Bedard, McDavid entered the league at 18. Edmonton Oilers fans expected him to be an all-time great player. McDavid lived up to those expectations. He led the NHL in scoring in his second season.

Sidney Crosby also debuted in the NHL at 18. The Pittsburgh Penguins star was one of Bedard's favorite players growing up. It didn't take long for Bedard to face off against Crosby.

During his NHL debut, Bedard skates by Sidney Crosby.

On October 10, 2023, Bedard made his NHL debut against the Penguins.

Chicago fell behind 2–0 in the game. But Bedard helped start a Blackhawks rally. He grabbed a loose puck and sent a no-look pass to teammate Alex Vlasic. Ryan Donato then

Bedard looks for an open teammate in a game during his rookie year.

scored on a rebound of Vlasic's shot. Bedard was credited with an assist for his first NHL point. Better still, the Blackhawks won their season opener 4–2.

Bedard adjusted to the NHL quickly. The night after his debut, Bedard scored against the Boston Bruins for his first NHL goal. In a game against the Tampa Bay Lightning, Bedard scored two goals and added two assists. He became the youngest player with four points in an NHL game since 1944.

The Blackhawks struggled to win games in 2023–24. But Bedard lived up to the hype. The phenom won the Calder Memorial Trophy that season. This award is given to the NHL's best rookie. Fans in Chicago were thrilled to watch a superstar in the making.

HISTORY REPEATING

Connor's great-great-uncle Jim Bedard had a brief NHL career in the 1940s and 1950s. He also played for Chicago. And just like Connor, he also scored his first NHL goal against Boston. However, Jim never scored another goal in his career.

TIMELINE

1. **North Vancouver, British Columbia (July 17, 2005)**
   Connor Bedard is born.

2. **Frisco, Texas (May 6, 2021)**
   In his first international tournament, Connor scores in the gold-medal game of the World Under-18 Championship. Canada goes on to win 5–3.

3. **Regina, Saskatchewan (April 17, 2022)**
   Connor scores his 50th goal of the season for the Regina Pats, becoming the youngest player in WHL history to reach 50 goals.

4. **Halifax, Nova Scotia (January 2, 2023)**
   Connor scores the game-winner in overtime as Canada beats Slovakia in the World Junior Championship. Canada goes on to win the gold medal three days later.

5. **Saskatoon, Saskatchewan (March 19, 2023)**
   Connor scores his 140th point of the 2022–23 season, becoming the first player since 1995–96 to record that many points in a WHL season.

6. **Nashville, Tennessee (June 28, 2023)**
   The Chicago Blackhawks pick Connor first overall in the NHL Entry Draft.

7. **Pittsburgh, Pennsylvania (October 10, 2023)**
   Bedard records an assist in his NHL debut.

MAP

1
5
3
4
7
6
2

AT A GLANCE

Birth date: July 17, 2005

Birthplace: North Vancouver, British Columbia

Position: Center

Shoots: Right

Size: 5-foot-10 (178 cm), 185 pounds (84 kg)

NHL team: Chicago Blackhawks (2023–)

Previous team: Regina Pats (2020–23)

Major awards: Calder Memorial Trophy (2024), World Junior Championship MVP (2023), Four Broncos Memorial Trophy (2023), Jim Piggott Memorial Trophy (2021)

Accurate through April 2025.

GLOSSARY

assisted
Made a pass, rebound, or deflection that resulted in a goal.

backhand
The outside of the stick blade.

debut
First appearance.

draft
An event that allows teams to choose new players coming into the league.

elite
The best of the best.

hat trick
When a player scores three or more goals in a game.

junior hockey
A level of hockey in which young players can improve their skills.

phenom
A person who is extremely talented at a young age.

rebound
When the goalie makes a save, but the puck goes back into play.

rookie
A first-year player.

stem cells
Cells that can divide and develop into more-specialized cells.

TO LEARN MORE

Books

Berglund, Bruce. *Hockey GOATs: The Greatest Athletes of All Time*. North Mankato, MN: Capstone Press, 2024.

Kortemeier, Todd. *Chicago Blackhawks*. Mendota Heights, MN: Press Box Books, 2023.

Wiseman, Blaine. *Stanley Cup*. New York: Lightbox Learning, 2024.

More Information

To learn more about Connor Bedard, go to **pressboxbooks.com/AllAccess**.

These links are routinely monitored and updated to provide the most current information available.

INDEX